nothing.
volume two.

quips.

nothing.
volume two.
adnan ali.

quips.

This is not a copyright page.
This is a Creative Commons Page.
Awwww, yeah!

Highly Adequate Press.
Adnan Ali, (cc) 2015. Some Rights Reserved.
Attribution-Noncommercial 3.0 Unported
http://creativecommons.org/licenses/by-nc/3.0/
(Apart from the images from the noun project, they are under their own licenses or public domain.)

You are free to copy, distribute and adapt this book (for noncommercial purposes and with proper attribution). I mean, I guess you could distribute this book for commercial purposes and without attribution if you really really wanted. But frankly, I don't think that would be very nice. I might come after you for doing so, but that depends on the day and my mood. It's available for free from the website below anyway, so, like... I don't know. I just wanted to share some ideas, you know?

The online version of this book can be found at
http://nothing.jaaduhai.com/volume-two/

*this one
is for me.*

You'll be delighted
to meet me,
I know I was.

I'm not saying that you're not a better person than I am. I am just trying to ascertain by

We, the idealists,
are the real realists.

When I grow up, I want to be younger.

I

less
than
three

you.

A colourless life
still has shades.

a metaphor
is like
a simile.

I don't know what you're thinking and why you'd think otherwise.

Laziness is the key to avoiding bad habits.

My opinions are better than yours and so are my facts.

A lot of what they teach in business school is bullshit,

turns out that bullshit is actually very useful in the business world.

There
are
no
spaces
between
spoken
words.

I don't like people liking people I don't like.

I can lie with a straight face or with my own face.

Irony
is the
best
policy.

People rave about home-cooked meals, but I've been to other people's homes and the food isn't that great.

For a moment I heard myself listening and it gave me further pause.

The facts don't lie, but sometimes they withhold the truth.

More than fair is unfair.

I'd love you to death, but I'm afraid it might kill you.

I am terrified,
it turns out, by
nearly everything.

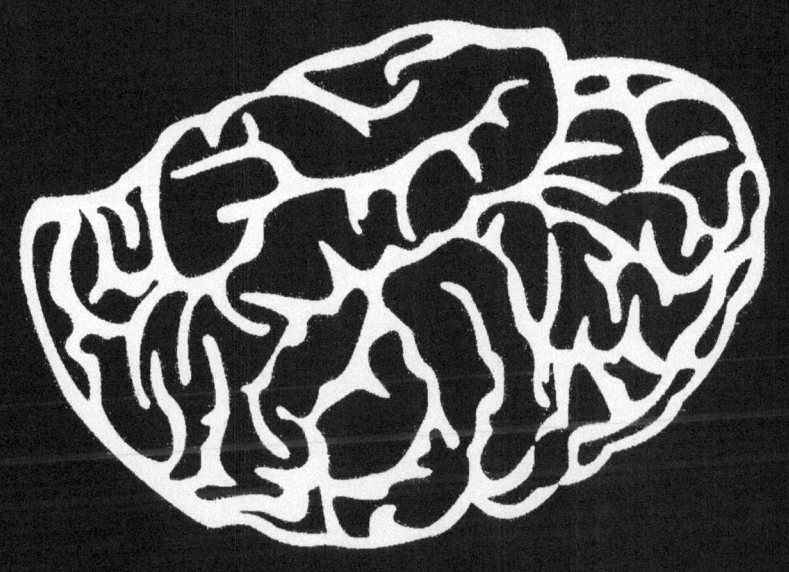

If I put my mind to it, there's nothing I could accomplish.

I don't know
when I am not.

Place us in the universe and we are microorganisms.

Opinions without pi are onions.

I can't even begin to pretend to have understood what you just said.

What is the difference between the moments you want to live to see and the moments you would die for?

You can't have your bakery and eat it, too.

I'm not one to take a situation into my own hands, unless it falls into my lap.

Your reputation precedes you; and with any luck, you will depart before it does.

That's not long enough to be a short story.

 Even time might not tell.

I think night school is a brilliant concept, if you have nothing to do during the day.

I'm funny beyond compare,
unless you compare me to
someone who's just as funny as
I am, or someone who's funnier.

You were missed, largely due to the lack of your presence.

We all need to get into a room and miscommunicate.

Love and be loved? Or live and let live?

Everything that happens could not have not happened.

May all your dreams come true...

on the same day.

 I was playing the world's smallest violin, and it broke.

It can't not work because it does primarily nothing.

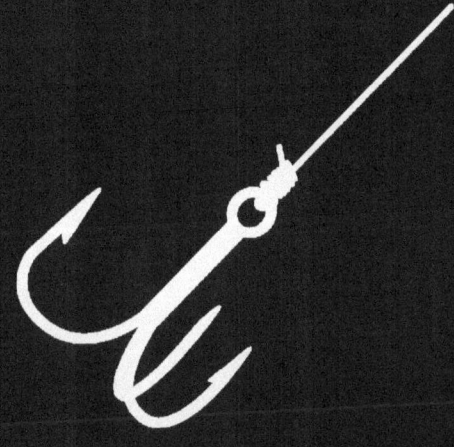

Humans fish for sheep.

One of the ways to be true to yourself is to be as vague as possible.

A wedding invitation is an invitation to a wedding, not an invitation to be wed.

I once made a
decision, but then
I undecided.

Short-term memory is the worst, just like long-term memory.

Wow, a train of thought, eh; I could fit all my thoughts into a mini.

All I ever wanted
was everything,

and everything else.

Awfully incredible or incredibly awful?

What doesn't kill me will only leave me severely hospitalized.

And before you know it, you will have climbed the mountain you were trying to move.

Whenever people say,
"it doesn't matter."
I say, "it matters to me."

And now it matters.

There ought to be a mirror
for every mask in the world.

Just give me a second, while I try to regain my passion for things.

What up's?

It is arguably no use spilling milk over people who are crying.

I do not forgive
and I do not forget.
Actually, that's not
true. Sometimes I do
forgive, but then I end
up forgetting that I've
forgiven.

A slow and painful death? Or a slow and painful life?

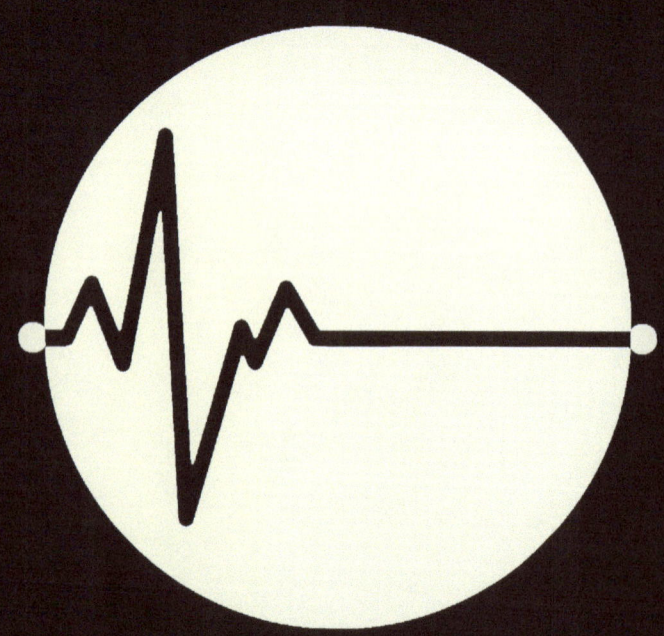

There
is
nothing
awkward
about
silence.

There is no undo button in life, but there is definitely a redo button.

Rome was also never not built.

I feel like my insult is being intelligenced.

Excellent timing is a virtue, patience is just luck.

Every now that you can know is past.

What I would actually do is irrelevant.
I am a philosopher not a saint.

False modesty is outright disingenuous. True humility is just plain boring.

I want to stereotype everyone but there are so many people.

The suspense is throwing salt on my wounds, but not killing me yet.

You can be loud without being sound.

"I knew you'd ask that question," is not the answer to my question.

I could care less,
and I will.

I miss my old problems, they were so easy to handle.

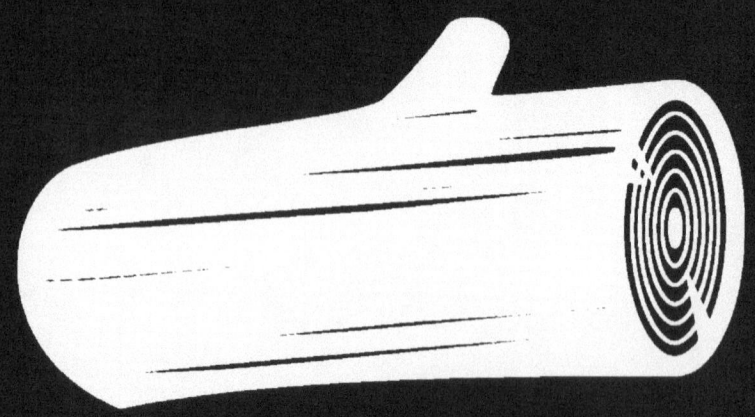

How much wood would
a woodchuck chuck
for minimum wage?

Even when the
moon is full all we
see is half.

Some sentences
end long before
the full stop, I hope
you get to the end
of this one.

It's the thought that counts, as long as it's expressed.

You have the eyes of the beholder.

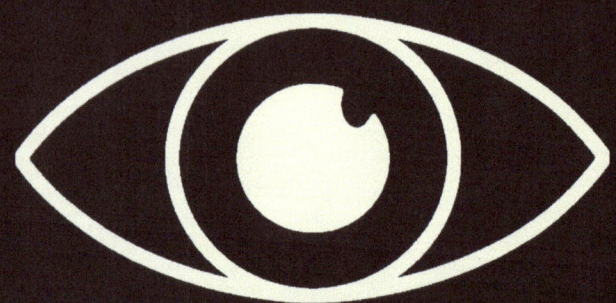

Where is there
nothing rather
than something?

When someone says that you're worth your weight in gold, they're saying that gold is worth more than you.

Everybody seems to know what nobody wants.

Wouldn't it be awesome if the universe would just collapse upon itself when someone orders an everything bagel?

Slowly you put on shades of comfort, leaving yourself naked.

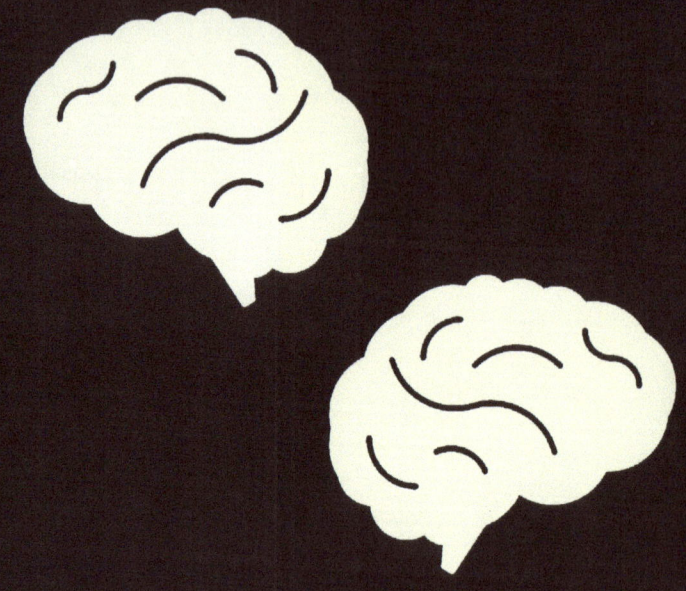

You should think twice before you think twice.

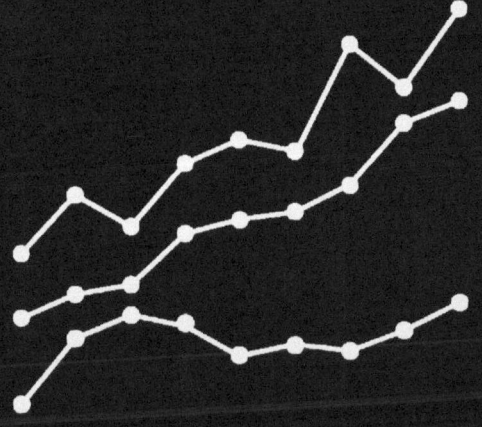

I clicked on a link that said "plot" expecting to see a graph but instead got a storyline.

I like to start each day by waking up.

I need to think of nothing; nothing doesn't worry me like everything else.

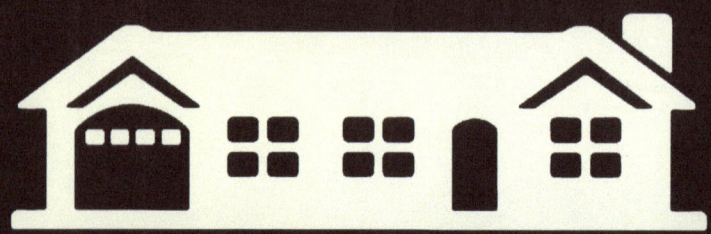

The weather man said, "Don't get your hopes up." As if he was forecasting my life.

Why must we clean the sink after we do the dishes?

Have we not suffered enough?

I said I was keeping it real, but I didn't say where.

There's two types of people here: those who're smart, and those who think they're smart.

What do you think you are?

Food for thought makes me hungrier.

They say that the best camera is the one that's with you. I'd like to remind everyone that there are much better cameras that are not with you.

Planning on going or going on planning?

If you had
nothing, what
would you
need?

The wolf doesn't care if you cry wolf in the wolf's part of town.

Late nights make mornings difficult.

I think I've been told I'm an awful listener.

I just called to say I tweeted.

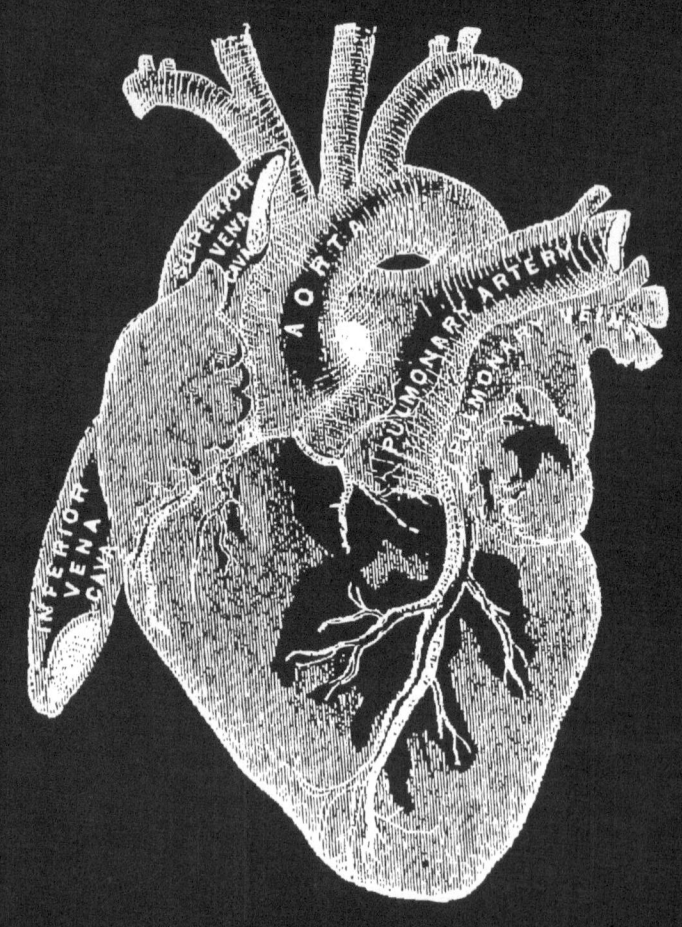

What I don't like about sadness is that I feel it in my heart.

We're not having an intelligent conversation... you aren't holding up your end of intelligent.

I *wish* objects in that mirror were closer than they appear to be.

liar, liar ...

your pants are also liars.

I don't think you understand how funny I was.

I dream therefore I desire –
I desire, therefore I am.

acknowledgments.

This book is happenstance, as is everything.

Most of the textual content in this book was posted to my blog. It dates as far back as July of 2003. So in a sense, this book has been over 10 years in the making. Whoa!

I want to give a shout out to my sister, Narjis Ali, who after seeing my notepad while we were waiting at a doctor's clinic asked me, "Where do you get these?" When I told her that I write these myself, she suggested something to the effect of, "You should sell these to a magazine or something!" While I never did do that, these words now, some 6 years after that conversation, appear in a book.

Of course, I want to thank my parents, Kauser and Mir Ghazanfar Ali. These are the same ones from volume one.

I want to thank my friends who helped with proof reading, etc: Sana Contractor and Iffat Sajjad. I also want to thank Alyona Polianskaia for her feedback on the physical drafts. This is a better book because of their help.

Like last time, I want to thank all the people who gave me feedback along the way. You are too numerous to name, so I will name you all here (minus those already named): Ron Ijack, Azadeh Mahinpou, Adeela Ahmad, Rahul Datta, Adam Doige, Wahiba Bukhari, Sana Rizvi, Tasneem Hussain, Petula Neale, Faiqa Khan, Noman Razi, Haaris Gilani, Sara Mir, Saira Aziz, Shazmeen Yusuf, Saifra Khan, Natalie Kotikova, Lara Callista, Basit Iqbal, Sahaj Cheema, Sathya Thillainathan and Patrick Lauria. Thank you all so very much (I pretty much copy pasted this from the last book).

Here it is, as if from nothing followed by billions of years. Once again, I hope that there is something here. And that you find it here.

notes and things.

A lot of these quips came about through actual conversation, sometimes face to face and sometimes virtual. I use and re-use some of them to this day.

The images in this book mostly come from The Noun Project (thenounproject.com) and are licensed to be used here. You can find a full attribution chart on the website for this book.

I want to share something with you. It is not meant as an objective observation, but rather it is something that I felt -- an emotional reaction. I did not feel it after completing the first book. But after having finished the draft of this book, I felt like I had created something beautiful. Which is not to say that this is a beautiful book. It is simply how I felt. The feeling itself is beautiful. It made me feel beautiful. It made me feel like I had something to offer to the world around me. I hope that you have the opportunity to experience this someday, if you have not already. I wish this for you over and over.

Yes, I know that not all of these quips are funny. If you feel that any of these are sad or evoke some other thoughts or emotions, it is meant to be that way. Please do not write to me about this.

The following page was left unintentionally blank. Really, there was nothing I could do about it.

those who make the extra turn,
make the world turn.

www.ingramcontent.com/pod-product-compliance
Lightning Source LLC
Chambersburg PA
CBHW042334150426
43194CB00005B/159